# The BBQ★BOOK

## BY DJ BBQ

PENGUIN BOOKS

PHOTOGRAPHY BY DAVID LOFTUS

# HI GUYS,
# JAMIE HERE!

I'm so excited to be introducing this brilliant barbecue cookbook – it's short, sweet and to the point, it's super-indulgent, and, most importantly, it's 50 of the best barbecue recipes that I'm confident you'll want to reach for every time you're cooking outdoors. From meat to fish to veggies, plus a whole range of useful tips and cooking techniques, you'll be amazed at what you can get out of your humble barbecue. The author of this book is the most fabulous, bonkers, charming guy, Mr Christian Stevenson aka DJ BBQ, and boy, what this fella can't do on the barbecue isn't worth knowing.

This little book is one of the first in a collection of no-nonsense, beautiful cookbooks, inspired by the incredible cooks, chefs and artisans on my Food Tube channel. If you don't know the channel already, hunt us out on YouTube, where myself and a bunch of super-talented people, including DJ BBQ, are uploading exclusive videos every week, with plenty of clever tips, tricks and methods that'll transform your cooking. We're a community of food lovers and experts, who simply want to share our passion with you guys, so if you have any questions, please leave a comment and we'll be happy to answer.

So back to this little beauty – with the recipes in this book, DJ BBQ's really fun videos on Food Tube and a little bit of his heart and soul, your barbecue will never be the same again. I'm sure you'll also learn some new words along the way from this crazy cat, but don't fight it – embrace it.

Big love,

youtube.com/jamieoliver

# WHAT UP EARTH?
## ★ I'M DJ BBQ ★

Welcome to my world of outdoor grilling. It's no secret that I like the taste of food much better when it's cooked over wood and charcoal – cooking over live fire brings out that inner caveman. It's primal, it's feral . . . it's rad. Plus, it's sociable!

For me, cooking on live fire harks back to times gone by when the charcoal makers were the wealthiest men around. If someone went out to rob a stagecoach, it'd be the charcoal makers they'd be after for a decent prize. Charcoal is part of a whole big story that makes cooking with it even more primitive, and it's becoming more and more relevant now, with charcoal producers experiencing a renaissance in the UK. If you only take one thing from this book, please let it be this – wherever possible, buy local, sustainably sourced coal.

My love affair with barbecuing started when I was eight years old. My parents split up and I went to live with my dad – he was OK in the kitchen, but better on the grill. He had learnt from his father, who was king of the grill. Grandpa would often load up the car with his four children, loads of food and his trusty barbecue, and they'd drive over the border of Iowa into the Dakotas, where they'd pull up at a state park and throw down an amazing barbecued picnic feast. Grandpa would have four chickens, a couple of racks of ribs, potatoes, sauces, corn – the whole works on his little transportable barbecue! He passed on the knowledge to my dad, who then got me on the grill from an early age. Man, I burnt hotdogs, hamburgers and steaks, until one time in particular when I was cutting the fat off a raw steak. Dad barked at me, 'What are you doing?' to which I responded, 'Cutting the fat off. I'm only gonna cut it off later when I'm eating it.' 'But that's where the flavour comes from, son,' Dad retorted. And this is how I learnt.

This book is full of recipes that I've cooked time and again during my 45 years of walking this earth. Many are family recipes and others are inspired by my travels, starting in Ocean City, Maryland, working for an old-school hippy called Woodstock Dan, to shredding the Rockies in Vail, Colorado, making snowboarding films and working at the 24-hour DJ's Diner, to spending my summers in Lagos, Portugal, during the 90s. Barbecuing is all about cooking for a crowd and that's what I love to do, so get some people round, make sure your beer is ice cold and fire up that grill!

# CONTENTS

## ★ ★ ★ ★ PARTY TIME ★ ★ ★ ★

## QUICK-FIRE GRILLS

# SLOW & LOW

# SIDES & SALADS

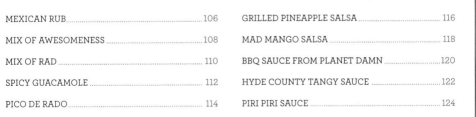

# RUBS, DIPS, SALSAS & SAUCES

# COOKING TECHNIQUES

HERE ARE MY DIFFERENT COOKING TECHNIQUES, WHERE YOU'LL LEARN TO BALANCE YOUR COOKING BETWEEN HOT, DIRECT HEAT AND THE LESS FIERCE, INDIRECT HEAT – THIS IS THE ART OF DIRECT VERSUS INDIRECT BARBECUING. I'VE GIVEN YOU A GUIDELINE TECHNIQUE IN ALL MY RECIPES, BUT YOU MIGHT FIND OTHER METHODS WORK BEST IF YOU'RE BARBECUING MORE THAN ONE THING AT A TIME – DON'T BE AFRAID TO TAKE CHANCES AND USE YOUR INSTINCTS. THE MORE YOU COOK, THE EASIER IT GETS.

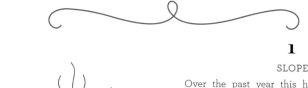

### 1

### SLOPE

Over the past year this has been one of my go-to techniques – it'll give you a nice range of heat to play with. Pile the coals up so you have loads on one side and none on the other, making sure there's a nice gradual slope in between.

### 2

### HALF & HALF

This does what it says on the tin and it's a great method if you want hot, direct heat but you also want a safe zone if things get a bit crazy. Set up the barbecue so half the base is covered in charcoal and the other side is empty.

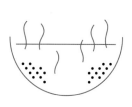

### 3

### HEAT CANYON

This is one of my favourite ways of cooking! Place the coals on opposite sides of the barbecue to make two heat walls – this will create sections of hot, direct heat on the sides, with an indirect, cooler area in the middle to ensure your meat gets consistent heat throughout the cook.

## 4
### LONELY ISLAND

This method is great when cooking hunks of meat slow and low over a long period of time. It's what I'd use to turn my standard kettle barbecue into a smoker (before I had a smoker, that is), so don't use this to do straightforward grilling. Place a small amount of charcoal in the corner of your barbecue so you have a little island of coals on one side, then cover with the lid and let it heat up.

A note for gas grills: I prefer to cook over live fire, but most of the recipes in this book will work using gas too – if you're looking to emulate the indirect method of barbecuing, turn on half the barbecue and place the hunk of meat on the cool side (you'll need a large barbecue for this). Close the lid to turn your gas grill into an outdoor oven.

★ ★ ★ ★ ★ ★ ★ ★ ★ ★ ★ ★ ★ ★ ★ ★ ★ ★ ★ ★ ★ ★ ★ ★ ★ ★ ★ ★ ★ ★ ★ ★ ★ ★ ★ ★ ★ ★ ★ ★ ★ ★ ★

## 🔥 LET'S GET HOT 🔥

To get the heat just right, the best advice I can give you is: GET TO KNOW YOUR BARBECUE. Your instincts are your best friend, but here are some tips to help you along the way too. When using your barbecue as an outdoor oven, play with the temperatures, by adjusting the vents and the amount of coals you add. I've given you ballpark temperatures that you should aim for – you can guesstimate and use your instincts, but having a temperature gauge or thermometer helps.

**For grilling, here's how I check the heat:** hold your hand about 12cm above the barbecue. Now count how many seconds you can comfortably keep your hand in place. Be careful and don't be some gnarly jackass dude and think you're invincible – be honest with your heat!

★ 6 seconds    low heat

★ 4 seconds    medium heat

★ 2 seconds    hotter than a goat's butt in a chilli pepper patch heat

★ 0 seconds    you might want to go to your nearest hospital

# MY BBQ TOP TIPS

THESE PAGES WILL HELP YOU SET UP YOUR BARBECUE TO ENSURE YOU GET THE MOST AWESOME RESULTS POSSIBLE:

## 1

Before you start, always make sure your barbecue is clean of any ash, grease or debris. You need oxygen to flow through it properly to create and maintain the correct heat.

## 2

A clean grill is important too – scrub the bars with a wire brush while they're still warm, then rub with half a lemon (or any other citrus fruit) to make them super-clean. Vinegar works well too, but please never use chemical products – they'll make your food taste nasty.

## 4

I really recommend buying a chimney starter – it's easy to use and such an efficient way of getting your coals red hot in no time, without having to use lighter fluid or blocks. Simply fill with charcoal, place a couple of scrunched-up balls of newspaper underneath and light them up. Once super-hot and grey, pour the coals on to the barbecue (see pages 10–11 for techniques) and you're ready to go. I recommend replenishing your barbecue with hot coals, instead of cold ones – this'll help the barbecue to maintain a steady, consistent heat throughout the cooking process.

## 3

Buy sustainably sourced lumpwood charcoal and, if possible, buy locally, both to support the economy and to do your bit for the planet by reducing your carbon footprint. Around 95% of the charcoal we use is imported, but I'm happy to say that locally produced charcoal is experiencing a renaissance as of late. I prefer cooking with lumpwood charcoal, but if you can only find briquettes, they work too. Try not to use ones that contain chemical binders, as they can taint the taste of your food if they're not completely grey before cooking.

## 5

You'll notice that I like to use wood chips to give meat a nice smoky flavour. As meat mainly absorbs that flavour for the first 3 hours or so, you'll never need more than a few handfuls for each cook. I use oak, hickory, or for a strong smoky taste, mesquite. I also like fruit woods, like apple, cherry and plum, for a sweeter smoky flavour. I mainly use wood chips or chunks for longer cooks, but don't be afraid to throw some on, even if you're doing a quick grill. Just remember, they need to be soaked for at least 30 minutes before using.

## 6

Tongs are essential – treat them as an extension of your hand. Invest in a couple of good-quality pairs – one for raw meat and one for cooked. An old oven glove is useful too.

## 8

To avoid flare-ups, always make sure you shake off any excess marinade or oil from anything you put on the barbecue – you don't want burnt food!

## 9

When using the barbecue like an outdoor oven, to check your food always carefully crack the lid open before lifting it off completely – this will prevent the ash from blowing up and tainting the flavour of your food.

## 7

I always place a drip tray in my barbecue on the indirect side to collect fat or grease from the food – this will help stop your barbecue getting clogged up. Even if you're only cooking over direct heat, you may need to move the food over to the indirect side if there are any flare-ups, so it's always good to use a drip tray to protect your barbecue. You can pick them up pretty cheaply, or just use an old roasting tray or a big piece of tin foil.

# PARTY TIME

Barbecuing is all about the social atmosphere. It's where people gather to drink, converse, laugh, and to grab a tasty, tender morsel off the grill.

# RAD RUM RIBS

★ ★ ★ ★  **SERVES 8**  ★ ★ ★ ★

**TOTAL TIME: 3 HOURS
PLUS MARINATING**

sea salt and freshly ground
black pepper

1.5kg baby back ribs,
membrane removed

**FOR THE PASTE**

5 tablespoons maple syrup

2 teaspoons chipotle chilli paste

1 tablespoon ground ginger

1 tablespoon Worcestershire sauce

1½ teaspoons sweet paprika

1½ teaspoons ground cumin

1 teaspoon Chinese five-spice

½ teaspoon ground nutmeg

**FOR THE RAD RUM BBQ SAUCE**

4cm piece of ginger, peeled

3–4 cloves of garlic, peeled

125ml tomato ketchup

60ml dark rum

1 tablespoon Worcestershire sauce

3 tablespoons cider vinegar

1 teaspoon Dijon mustard

½ teaspoon dried chilli flakes

50g soft dark brown sugar

Combine the paste ingredients and 2 teaspoons of salt in a bowl. Pat the ribs dry with kitchen paper, then place in a tray and rub all over with the paste. Cover with clingfilm and leave to marinate in the fridge for at least 6 hours, or preferably overnight.

When you want to cook, remove the ribs from the fridge, shake off any excess marinade and allow to come up to room temperature. Meanwhile, set up your barbecue for the half and half technique (see page 10) – you want a medium indirect heat. Place a drip tray inside the barbecue on the indirect side. Cover with the lid and allow to heat up like an outdoor oven – you want a temperature of around 180°C/350°F.

Rip off just over an arm's length of extra-strong tin foil, stack up the ribs in the centre and tightly wrap. Place the foil parcel over indirect heat on the barbecue, cover with the lid and cook for around 2 hours, or until the meat is tender and starts to fall away from the bone, remembering to replenish with hot coals every 45 minutes or so. Meanwhile, finely grate the ginger and garlic into a small pan on the hob. Add the rest of the BBQ sauce ingredients and 80ml of water. Simmer over a medium heat for around 20 minutes, or until thickened, stirring occasionally. Season to taste and set aside.

Remove the ribs from the foil and brush all over with the BBQ sauce and any cooking juices. Return to the indirect heat for another 30 to 40 minutes with the lid on, or until tender and golden, basting well every 10 minutes or so. Remove to a board to rest for 5 minutes, then carve. Enjoy, 'cause these ribs rule!

> My mate Tim got me into this way of cooking ribs. He started with bourbon then we experimented with rum. I loved his version so started making my own tweaks and now we have . . . rad rum ribs.

16

# CHERRY WOOD SMOKED CHICKEN

**SERVES 6**

TOTAL TIME: 1 HOUR 45 MINUTES

1 x 1.7kg higher-welfare
whole chicken

1 x **mix of awesomeness**
(see page 108)

½ a lemon

½ an orange

YOU NEED

soaked cherry wood chips
(roughly 200g)

Remove the chicken from the fridge to come up to room temperature. Meanwhile, set up your barbecue for the heat canyon technique (see page 10). Place a drip tray inside the middle of the barbecue. Cover with the lid and allow to heat up like an outdoor oven – you want a temperature of around 175°C/345°F.

Rub the **mix of awesomeness** really well all over the chicken, then shove the lemon and orange halves into the cavity. Sprinkle a good handful of wood chips over the hot coals, then place the bird on the middle of the barbecue and cover with the lid. Cook for around 1 hour 30 minutes, or until golden and cooked through. Replenish with hot coals halfway, if needed, and sprinkle over some wood chips twice more throughout the cooking process, but try not to keep the lid off for too long as you'll let all the heat out.

To check if the bird is ready, pierce a thigh with a knife – if the juices run clear, it's done. Take it off to rest for 10 minutes, then carve up and enjoy those sweet, smoky flavours. Serve as part of a big spread with rice, buttery new potatoes and a load of salads.

The problem with this dish is the jealousy you'll incur if you post photos of it on social media – it's one of the tastiest, most good-looking things you'll ever cook. If you can't get hold of cherry wood, other fruit woods will give you that sweet, smoky flavour too.

# KICK-ASS FISH TACOS

**TOTAL TIME: 25 MINUTES**

1 x **mad mango salsa** (see page 118)

1 x **spicy guacamole** (see page 112)

½ a small red cabbage (400g)

3 tablespoons cider or
white wine vinegar

600g tilapia, halibut or other
firm white fish fillets

1 tablespoon **Mexican rub**
(see page 106)

16 small soft corn tortillas

Before you set up the barbecue, make sure the bars of the grill are really clean and well oiled. Set it up for the half and half technique (see page 10) – you want a medium direct heat. Place a drip tray inside the barbecue on the indirect side. While that's heating up, get the **mad mango salsa** and **spicy guacamole** ready to go, then really finely slice the cabbage and mix well in a bowl with the vinegar.

Rinse the fish fillets under cold running water, then drain, pat dry and sprinkle over the **Mexican rub**. Place the fillets over direct heat on the barbecue (I like to pop them into a greased fish basket to help prevent the fillets from falling apart). Cook for 4 minutes, or until cooked through, turning halfway – the thickness of the fillets will affect the cooking time, so use your common sense and adjust the time accordingly. Meanwhile, either divide the tortillas into two stacks of eight, wrap each in a double layer of tin foil and warm through on the barbecue for a couple of minutes, or griddle them in a pan on the barbecue with a drizzle of oil for 15 seconds on each side.

Remove the fillets and flake into big beautiful chunks. I divide them between the tortillas with a dollop of spicy guacamole and a spoonful each of cabbage and mad mango salsa, but each to their own. Hells to the yeah to the power of Ep-Gnar!*

Fish tacos are one of my all-time favourite meals. I've never found a restaurant in the UK that would do this dish the way I've had 'em in the US, so I learnt how to do it myself and here it is for you.

*Ep-Gnar is the ultimate union of epic and gnarly.

# NAYA'S PIZZA DOUGH & TOMATO SAUCE

SERVES
4

TOTAL TIME: 30 MINUTES
PLUS PROVING

FOR THE DOUGH

500g plain flour

300g strong white bread flour

2 teaspoons Himalayan pink
or fine sea salt

1 x 7g sachet of fast-action yeast

2 tablespoons runny honey

120ml olive oil

FOR THE TOMATO SAUCE

1 medium onion, peeled

2 tablespoons olive oil

3 cloves of garlic, peeled

sea salt and freshly ground
black pepper

½ a small bunch of fresh basil,
leaves picked

500ml passata or 1 x 400g
tin of chopped tomatoes

1 teaspoon dried oregano

To make the dough, put 450ml of lukewarm water and the dough ingredients (excluding the oil) into the bowl of an electric mixer (or a large regular bowl if using a hand-mixer). Mix on a low speed for 1 minute, then scrape down the sides and give it another blast. Keep mixing on a low speed as you slowly add the oil, then mix for a further 5 to 7 minutes so you end up with a slightly wet, smooth and elastic dough. Transfer to a lightly greased bowl, cover with a damp tea towel and set aside to prove in a warm place for 1 hour, or until doubled in size.

Meanwhile, make the tomato sauce. Finely chop the onion and fry in a medium pan over a medium-low heat with the oil for around 5 minutes, or until softened but not coloured. Crush in the garlic with a pinch of salt and pepper for another minute. Finely chop and add the basil leaves along with the passata or chopped tomatoes, and the oregano. Either whiz it up with a stick blender or keep it chunky, then set aside.

Once risen, gently knock the dough back on a flour-dusted surface, then equally divide and roll it into 4 rounds (roughly 20cm in diameter and 3mm thick). Now you're ready to choose your toppings and create whatever awesome pizza creation you like. Turn the page for more details on how I like to do it …

> I have my wife, Naya, to thank for this recipe –
> she is the queen of dough! You can freeze any
> leftover tomato sauce and use it for more pizzas
> and calzoni, or stirred through pasta.

# PIZZA

**COOKING TIME: 10 MINUTES PER PIZZA**

Set up your barbecue for the heat canyon technique (see page 10), cover with the lid and allow to heat up like an outdoor oven – you want a temperature of around 230°C/450°F. Spread 1 tablespoon of **tomato sauce** (see page 22) on each dough round (see page 22), tear over some **mozzarella cheese** and add your favourite toppings. I like **pepperoni**, finely sliced **mushrooms** and **red onion**, a few torn **fresh basil leaves** and a good drizzling of **olive oil**. Dust a pizza stone or a large metal roasting tray with plenty of **semolina flour**, place a pizza on top and cook on the barbecue with the lid on for 10 to 12 minutes, or until golden, crisp and the cheese has melted. Repeat with the remaining pizzas, slicing them up and serving as you go. When my kids are done with their pizza, I always give them a pot of honey to dip their crusts into – it's like an instant dessert after every slice.

# CALZONE

SERVES 4

COOKING TIME: 15 MINUTES PER CALZONE

Set up your barbecue for the heat canyon technique (see page 10), cover with the lid and allow to heat up like an outdoor oven – you want a temperature of around 230°C/450°F. Spread 1 tablespoon of the **tomato sauce** (see page 22) over the surface of each dough round (see page 22), leaving a 2cm gap around the edge, then sprinkle your favourite fillings over one half – I like plenty of torn **mozzarella cheese**, some roasted **cherry tomatoes** and torn-up **prosciutto**. Fold the dough up and over the filling, pressing the edges together to seal. Dust a pizza stone or a large metal roasting tray with plenty of **semolina flour**, place a calzone on top and cook on the barbecue with the lid on for around 15 minutes, or until golden and cooked through. Repeat with the remaining calzoni, serving them up as you go. I always serve these with a bowl of warm leftover tomato sauce on the side, for dipping.

# JALAPEÑO PARTY POPPERS

★ ★ ★ ★  **SERVES 4**  ★ ★ ★ ★

**TOTAL TIME: 35 MINUTES**

16 fresh jalapeño chillies

½ a bunch of fresh coriander, leaves picked

2 spring onions, trimmed

75g Monterey Jack or Cheddar cheese

100g cream cheese

1 teaspoon smoked paprika

sea salt and freshly ground black pepper

8 rashers of higher-welfare smoked streaky bacon

**YOU NEED**

16 cocktail sticks

Set up your barbecue for the half and half technique (see page 10) – you want a medium direct heat. Place a drip tray inside the barbecue on the indirect side.

Wearing gloves, cut a slit lengthways down each chilli, then carefully make a T-cut at the stem end, leaving the stems intact. Using a teaspoon, scrape out and discard the seeds. Roughly chop the coriander leaves, finely chop the spring onions and put both into a bowl. Coarsely grate in the cheese, then add the cream cheese, paprika and a pinch of salt and pepper. Mix well, then carefully spoon equal portions of the mixture into the chillies. Halve the bacon rashers, then squeeze each chilli shut with your fingers and wrap a piece of bacon around each one, securing it in place with a cocktail stick.

Place the chillies over the direct heat on the barbecue and cook for around 10 minutes, or until lightly charred and the cheese is nice and oozy, turning halfway. Allow to cool for a few minutes before serving – and watch out for the super-spicy ones!

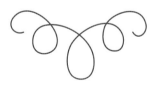

# SWEET POTATO QUESADILLAS

SERVES
6

**TOTAL TIME: 1 HOUR 45 MINUTES**

2 large sweet potatoes (roughly 800g), scrubbed clean

1 red or green pepper, deseeded

1 medium onion, peeled

2 cloves of garlic, peeled

1 fresh red chilli, deseeded

olive oil

½ a bunch of fresh coriander, leaves picked

150g feta or blue cheese

sea salt

12 medium flour tortillas

250g Monterey Jack or Cheddar cheese

**TO SERVE**

soured cream

your favourite salsa

Start by cooking the sweet potatoes: I tend to smoke them (see **mega stuffed sweet potatoes**, page 94, for instructions) or roast them in the oven at 180°C/350°F/gas 4 for around 45 minutes, or until soft in the middle. Allow them to cool, then scoop the flesh into a large bowl and mash well.

Set up your barbecue for the half and half technique (see page 10) – you want a medium-high direct heat. Meanwhile, finely chop the pepper, onion, garlic and chilli. Once the barbecue is hot, place a cast-iron frying pan over the direct heat with 1 tablespoon of oil. Fry the onion and pepper for a few minutes, then add the garlic and chilli. Continue frying for a further 5 minutes, or until softened, stirring occasionally. Remove from the heat and stir into the sweet potato bowl, then finely chop and add the coriander leaves. Crumble in the feta or blue cheese and add a good pinch of salt, then mix well to combine. Divide the mixture between 6 tortillas, then spread it out to the edges so the tortillas are nicely covered. Grate over the Monterey Jack or Cheddar cheese, then sandwich the remaining tortillas on top.

Wipe the pan clean and return to the barbecue. Once hot, carefully place a quesadilla in the pan, cover with the barbecue lid and bake for about 5 minutes, or until the cheese melts, turning halfway with a fish slice. You can also cook them over indirect heat on the bars of the grill if you prefer, just be quick flipping them over! When done, wrap in tin foil to keep warm while you cook the remaining quesadillas, then cut them all into wedges and serve immediately with soured cream and salsa. My kids love these (who doesn't?) – I tend to make them first thing in the morning and wrap them up as a treat for the kids' packed lunches.

# BEER CAN CHICKEN

SERVES
6

TOTAL TIME: 1 HOUR 50 MINUTES

1 x 1.7kg higher-welfare
whole chicken

4 sprigs of fresh rosemary

olive oil

sea salt and freshly ground
black pepper

1 x 330ml can of your favourite beer

> Once the chicken is
> cooked and resting, put
> some sunglasses on her
> and upload the photos
> to Instagram – a bird
> sitting on a can of beer
> in glasses will definitely
> get you some likes.

Before you start, check if your barbecue lid fits over the chicken upright. If not, don't worry, you can lay the bird out flat – you just need to decide which way you're doing it before you prepare the chicken, then set the bird aside to come up to room temperature. Meanwhile, set up your barbecue for the heat canyon technique (see page 10). Place a drip tray inside the middle of the barbecue. Cover with the lid and allow to heat up like an outdoor oven – you want a temperature of around 175°C/345°F.

Pick the leaves from 2 rosemary sprigs and bash in a pestle and mortar with a drizzle of oil and a good pinch of salt and pepper, then rub all over the chicken. Make sure the beer is at room temperature, then pour out two-thirds of it (or drink it!) and insert the remaining rosemary sprigs into the can. Now for the tricky bit – use both hands to pull the chicken's rear apart and carefully manoeuvre it on to the beer can. If you're laying the chicken flat, make sure you position the can so the hole is at the top to prevent the beer from spilling out.

Place the bird upright on the middle of the barbecue, making sure the legs are pointing forward so it doesn't topple over – a comical sight – and cover with the lid. Cook for around 1 hour 30 minutes, or until golden and cooked through, remembering to replenish with hot coals halfway, if needed. To check if it's ready, pierce a thigh with a knife – if the juices run clear, it's done. Remove the bird to a board to rest for 10 minutes (this is the perfect time to take some rad photos), then carve up and serve. Enjoy the juiciness, ness, ness . . . wow, this meal comes with reverb.

# MARYLAND SMOKED HOME FRIES

TOTAL TIME: 45 MINUTES

4 leftover smoked potatoes
(see **super-duper triply awesome smoked potatoes**, page 96)

optional: 100g chorizo

1 medium onion, peeled

1 red pepper, deseeded

8 closed cup or chestnut mushrooms

1 clove of garlic, peeled

vegetable oil

2 sprigs of fresh rosemary, leaves picked

sea salt and freshly ground black pepper

Set up your barbecue for the half and half technique (see page 10) – you want a high direct heat. Cut the smoked potatoes into 2.5cm chunks and slice the chorizo (if using). Roughly chop the onion and pepper, then thickly slice the mushrooms and finely slice the garlic. Place a large cast-iron frying pan over the heat – the water from the veg can stop the spuds turning golden, so you'll need a pretty ding dong dang big pan to cook everything at the same time, in their own separate zones.

Start by cooking the chorizo for about 5 minutes, or until golden and crispy, then remove to a plate, leaving that lovely oil behind. Swirl a good lug of vegetable oil around the pan and once hot, chuck in the potatoes for about 5 minutes, or until turning golden underneath, then stir and push to one side of the pan. Add another drizzle of oil to the empty space, followed by the chopped veg, garlic and rosemary leaves, keeping them apart from the potatoes. Cook for 15 minutes, or until the potatoes are golden, the veg are soft and any liquid has evaporated, stirring occasionally. Now you can start the party – mix everything up and stir in the crispy chorizo (if using). Cook for another couple of minutes until everything is golden, then season to taste. Awesome served with an over-easy fried egg on top.

I grew up in Maryland and have always eaten different versions of this from my grandmother and my pops, so here's mine. It's a great dinner with friends, eaten straight from the pan, but it's also my favourite meal to start the day. Just remember to take out the garlic – that's never nice in the morning! You can also cook this on the hob, if you prefer.

# PARTY-TIME CHICKEN FAJITAS

★ ★ ★ ★  SERVES 6  ★ ★ ★ ★

TOTAL TIME: 1 HOUR
PLUS MARINATING

6 x 150g higher-welfare
chicken breasts

3–4 tablespoons **Mexican rub**
(see page 106)

1 x 330ml can of your favourite beer

2 large onions, peeled

4 mixed-colour peppers, deseeded

100g closed cup or
chestnut mushrooms

12 medium flour tortillas

optional: olive oil

TO SERVE

1 x **spicy guacamole** (see page 112)

soured cream

1 x **pico de rado** (see page 114)

2 limes

YOU NEED

soaked wood chips (roughly 100g)

In a large bowl, give the chicken breasts a nice spicy massage in the **Mexican rub** and beer. Cover with clingfilm and leave to marinate in the fridge for at least 3 hours.

Drain and pat the chicken dry and allow to come up to room temperature. Meanwhile, set up your barbecue for the half and half technique (see page 10) – you want a medium-high direct heat. Place a drip tray inside the barbecue on the indirect side.

Finely slice the onions, peppers and mushrooms. Sprinkle a good handful of wood chips on to the hot coals, then place the chicken and veg over the direct heat – I use a griddle plate for the veg to stop them falling through the bars, but you can use a griddle pan on the hob if you don't have one. Cook for 10 to 12 minutes, or until the chicken is golden and cooked through and the veg are soft and slightly charred, turning halfway (if things get crazy, move everything to the indirect heat and cover with the lid until the chicken is cooked through). Meanwhile, either divide the tortillas into two stacks of six, wrap each in a double layer of tin foil and warm through on the barbecue for a couple of minutes, or griddle them in a pan on the barbecue with a drizzle of oil for 15 seconds on each side.

Slice up the chicken and paint the tortillas with **spicy guacamole** and soured cream. Let your friends layer up their own fajitas with the charred veg, chicken and **pico de rado**. Squeeze over some lime juice, roll up and chomp them!

Back in '92, my back porch was on the 11th tee of the Eagle Vail Golf Course. Please don't tell them, but we had midnight golf parties and ate these fajitas. We bought special golf balls that held a glow stick and would shove a flashlight upside down in the hole to flag it up. Good times, good food and a keg of cold beer. Now go try that 5 iron on the 11th tee.

# QUICK-FIRE GRILLS

This style of cooking goes hand in hand with burgers and dogs, but there's so much more you can do on your grill. I reckon these 10 recipes could bring about world peace.

# BALLISTIC
# BBQ CHICKEN

**TOTAL TIME: 1 HOUR PLUS BRINING**

4 higher-welfare chicken thighs

4 higher-welfare chicken drumsticks

1 x **mix of awesomeness** (see page 108)

**FOR THE BRINE**

3 tablespoons brown sugar or maple syrup

1 teaspoon cayenne pepper

2 teaspoons onion granules

2 teaspoons garlic granules

4 tablespoons sea salt

1 tablespoon freshly ground black pepper

Start by making the brine – this will help keep the meat juicy while it cooks. On the hob, warm 375ml of water in a medium pan over a low heat. Stir in all the brine ingredients and simmer for a few minutes, or until the salt dissolves, stirring occasionally. Remove from the heat and pour into a large bowl, then stir in 250ml of cold water and cool in the fridge for an hour. Once cooled, add the chicken thighs and drumsticks, then cover with clingfilm and return to the fridge for at least 4 hours, or preferably overnight.

When you want to cook, drain the chicken, then pat dry with kitchen paper and allow them to come up to room temperature. Meanwhile, set up your barbecue for the heat canyon technique (see page 10). Place a drip tray inside the middle of the barbecue. Cover with the lid and allow to heat up like an outdoor oven – you want a temperature of around 190°C/375°F.

Rub the **mix of awesomeness** all over the chicken thighs and drumsticks and place over indirect heat on the barbecue, then cover with the lid and cook for 35 to 40 minutes, or until cooked through. To check if it's ready, pierce a thigh with a knife – if the juices run clear, it's done. Using clean tongs, remove the chicken pieces to a board, cover with tin foil and leave to rest for 10 minutes, then serve and watch the angels sing.

# IOWA FLANK SKIRT STEAK

TOTAL TIME: 20 MINUTES
PLUS MARINATING

4 x 400g flank skirt steaks

2 x 300ml bottles of your favourite Italian dressing (or make your own by mixing 200ml olive oil, 100ml white wine vinegar, some chopped fresh soft herbs and a pinch of sea salt and freshly ground black pepper)

**YOU NEED**

4 sealable sandwich bags

This is the taste of home for me, and the best thing my father makes me. He's from the west coast of Iowa and whenever I visit him, he always has two or three flank skirt steaks marinating in the fridge, waiting for my arrival. It doesn't get better than this!

Put each steak into a sealable sandwich bag and divide the dressing between them – the vinegar within it helps to tenderize the meat and this is a tough cut, so marinating is essential. Massage the steaks to distribute the flavour (work it in, baby!), then throw those bags of magic into the fridge to marinate overnight (my dad sometimes leaves them in there for two nights to really work up the flavours and make them super-tender).

When you want to cook, remove the steaks from the sandwich bags, shake off any excess marinade and allow them to come up to room temperature. Set up your barbecue for the half and half technique (see page 10) – you want a high direct heat. Place a drip tray inside the barbecue on the indirect side. Once hot, place the steaks over the direct heat on the barbecue and cook for 8 to 10 minutes on each side – this cut of steak is a lot thicker in the middle, so it'll often be rarer in the middle and more cooked at the ends. If you're catering for lots of people who like their steak done differently, this'll please everyone. My step-mom likes it medium-rare, I like medium and my dad likes well-done, so with this dish we all always come up trumps. I find it's a more tender steak if you cook it to medium or medium-well.

Transfer the steaks to a board and leave to rest for 5 minutes, before slicing against the grain at a slight angle (I like fairly thin slices). Make sure you save the slices from each end for someone special – this is the most flavoursome part and rarely makes it to the table in my house. Serve with baked potatoes and a green salad.

# SCALLOPS
## WITH CHILLI GARLIC BUTTER

SERVES
2

TOTAL TIME: 20 MINUTES

12 scallops, trimmed, with
the shells (see tip below)

100ml dry white wine

½ a bunch of fresh flat-leaf parsley,
leaves picked

FOR THE CHILLI GARLIC BUTTER

2 tablespoons olive oil

100g salted butter

3 cloves of garlic, peeled

1 fresh red chilli

1 teaspoon freshly ground
black pepper

Spread hot coals over the base of your barbecue in a flat and even layer – the scallops are going to be cooked directly on the coals, so it doesn't matter what barbecue technique you use here.

Start by making the chilli garlic butter, which you can do on the barbecue or over a medium heat on the hob – basically the longer those flavours get to hang out together, the better. Place the oil and butter in a pan to melt. Meanwhile, finely chop the garlic and chilli (keep the seeds in if you like the heat), then add to the pan with the black pepper. Give it a good stir, let all the ingredients party, then set aside.

Place the shells with the scallops inside them on a platter, then add a dash of white wine to each one. Using tongs, place each shell directly on the grey coals, carefully positioning them so they can't tip over. Cover with the lid like an outdoor oven and cook for 4 to 6 minutes, or until cooked through, turning the scallops halfway with tongs. Carefully remove the shells to a serving platter and drizzle about 1 tablespoon of the melted chilli garlic butter over each golden scallop. Roughly chop and scatter over the parsley leaves then serve right away.

Ask your fishmonger to prep and clean the scallops for you. You'll be cooking them in their shells, so make sure you ask for these too.

# BODACIOUS BURGERS

TOTAL TIME: 30 MINUTES

500g beef mince

2 teaspoons English mustard powder

sea salt and freshly ground
black pepper

2 Portobello mushrooms

1 clove of garlic

olive oil

75g Monterey Jack or
Cheddar cheese

4 burger buns

1 round lettuce

1 large ripe tomato

Set up your barbecue for the half and half technique (see page 10) – you want a medium-high direct heat. Place a drip tray inside the barbecue on the indirect side.

Meanwhile, in a bowl mix the mince and mustard powder with a good pinch of salt and pepper, then shape into four equal-sized patties and season well on both sides. Slice each mushroom horizontally into two rounds, then halve the clove of garlic and rub all over. Drizzle with oil and season, then place the patties and mushrooms over the direct heat on the barbecue and cook for 8 to 10 minutes, or until the mushrooms are soft and cooked through, turning everything halfway – this will give you medium burgers, but feel free to adjust the cooking time so they're cooked to your liking. A couple of minutes before the burgers are done, grate the cheese and sprinkle on top, then put the lid on the barbecue to allow the cheese to get all oozy and melty.

Remove the burgers and mushrooms to a board to rest, then halve the burger buns and toast over direct heat for about 30 seconds. Click off a few lettuce leaves and divide between the toasted buns, then slice the tomato and place a round on each. Layer up the cheesy bodacious burgers and garlicky mushrooms, then add a dollop of ketchup (or not), before putting on the bun tops and tucking in to one of those beautiful babies.

# AWESOMEATRON LAMB LOIN CHOPS

SERVES
6

TOTAL TIME: 30 MINUTES

12 lamb loin chops

1 mixed bunch of fresh
rosemary, sage and thyme

olive oil

3 tablespoons **mix of rad**
(see page 110)

FOR THE DIPPING SAUCE

½ teaspoon cumin seeds

½ a bunch of fresh coriander,
leaves picked

350g 0% fat Greek yoghurt

1 teaspoon Dijon mustard

juice from ½ a lemon

100ml sweet chilli sauce

sea salt and freshly ground
black pepper

Remove the chops from the fridge to come up to room temperature. Meanwhile, set up your barbecue for the half and half technique (see page 10) – you want a medium-high direct heat. Place a drip tray inside the barbecue on the indirect side.

Make a herb basting brush by tying the stalky ends of the herbs around the handle end of a wooden spoon, making sure they're tightly secured. Combine 50ml of oil and 2 tablespoons of **mix of rad** in a bowl. Sprinkle the remaining mix of rad directly on to the chops, then place over the direct heat on the barbecue. Dip the herb brush into your tasty rad concoction and brush all over the meat, being careful not to use too much at once to avoid the coals flaring up. Cook for 10 to 12 minutes for medium-rare, or longer if you prefer, turning halfway and remembering to baste every few minutes. If you get some big flare-ups, simply move the meat to the cooler side of the barbecue until they subside.

Remove the chops to a board to rest for a few minutes. Meanwhile, make the dipping sauce. Gently toast the cumin seeds in a pan over a medium-high heat on the hob or on the barbecue for 1 to 2 minutes, or until golden, then grind to a fine powder in a pestle and mortar. Finely chop the coriander leaves and put into a bowl with the ground cumin, yoghurt, mustard, lemon juice and chilli sauce. Stir to combine, season to taste, then serve alongside your awesomeatron lamb loin chops. Now get dunking.

# MY MEAN MONKFISH KEBABS

**SERVES 6**

**TOTAL TIME: 40 MINUTES
PLUS MARINATING**

1 clove of garlic, peeled

2 unwaxed lemons

½ a bunch of fresh thyme,
leaves picked

sea salt and freshly ground
black pepper

olive oil

1kg monkfish fillets, skin and
sinew removed

1 x 180g piece of higher-welfare
thick pancetta (see tip below)

1 bunch of asparagus (300g)

200g ripe cherry tomatoes

**TO SERVE**

unsalted butter

lemon wedges

**YOU NEED**

12 metal or soaked wooden skewers

Before you set up the barbecue, make sure the bars of the grill are really clean and well oiled. Set it up for the half and half technique (see page 10) – you want a medium-high direct heat. Place a drip tray inside the barbecue on the indirect side.

Meanwhile, to make the marinade, crush the garlic into a pestle and mortar, add the zest from 2 lemons and the juice from 1, along with the thyme leaves, a good pinch of salt and pepper and a lug of oil, then bruise and bash into a paste. Cut the monkfish into 2cm chunks and slice the pancetta 1cm thick. Snap off and discard the woody ends of the asparagus, then cut the stalks into three equal pieces. Divide up the monkfish, pancetta, asparagus and tomatoes and thread on to the skewers, then place on a tray. Generously brush over the marinade, then cover and marinate in the fridge for at least 15 minutes.

Remove the kebabs from the fridge and shake off any excess marinade, then place on the direct heat on the barbecue (I like to pop them into a greased fish basket to make them really easy to handle). Grill for 6 to 8 minutes, or until cooked through, turning every couple of minutes. Serve the kebabs with a drizzling of melted butter and lemon wedges for squeezing over.

> You can find nice thick pancetta at your butchers, but if you can't get it simply wrap thin pancetta or streaky bacon around the asparagus pieces before skewering instead.

# CANDIED PORK FILLET

  **SERVES 4**

TOTAL TIME: 50 MINUTES
PLUS MARINATING

olive oil

125ml low-salt soy sauce

4 tablespoons dark brown sugar

4 cloves of garlic, bashed
and peeled

1 x 500g piece of higher-welfare
pork fillet

Make a marinade by putting a couple of lugs of oil and the soy sauce into a bowl, then stirring in the sugar until it dissolves. Chuck in the garlic cloves and pork, cover with clingfilm and marinate in the fridge for at least 2 hours, or preferably overnight.

When you want to cook, remove the pork from the fridge, shake off any excess marinade and allow to come up to room temperature. Meanwhile, set up your barbecue for the heat canyon technique (see page 10) – you want a medium-high direct heat. Place a drip tray inside the middle of the barbecue. Place the pork over direct heat on the barbecue for a couple of minutes, then turn and continue searing the meat for a few more minutes, or until browned all over. Move the pork to the middle of the barbecue, then cover with the lid like an outdoor oven and cook for 25 to 30 minutes, or until cooked through, turning every so often for a nice even colour.

Remove the pork to a board to rest so it stays juicy, then slice it up and watch people go nuts. If by some miracle there are any leftovers, this makes excellent sandwiches the next day.

✳ ✳ ✳ ✳ ✳ ✳ ✳ ✳ ✳ ✳ ✳ ✳ ✳ ✳ ✳ ✳ ✳ ✳ ✳ ✳ ✳ ✳ ✳ ✳ ✳ ✳ ✳ ✳ ✳ ✳ ✳ ✳ ✳ ✳

I promise that if you're cooking for a load of people, this will be the first thing that goes. My kids came up with the name and are always stoked when we make it – there's no candy, but we do use a bit of sugar for nice sweet meat.

✳ ✳ ✳ ✳ ✳ ✳ ✳ ✳ ✳ ✳ ✳ ✳ ✳ ✳ ✳ ✳ ✳ ✳ ✳ ✳ ✳ ✳ ✳ ✳ ✳ ✳ ✳ ✳ ✳ ✳ ✳ ✳ ✳ ✳

# PIRI PIRI CHICKEN WINGS

**SERVES 2-4**

TOTAL TIME: 1 HOUR 10 MINUTES

12 higher-welfare chicken wings

4 tablespoons **mix of awesomeness**
(see page 108)

1 x **piri piri sauce**
(see page 124)

Remove the wings from the fridge to come up to room temperature. Meanwhile, set up your barbecue for the heat canyon technique (see page 10). Place a drip tray inside the middle of the barbecue. Cover with the lid and allow to heat up like an outdoor oven – you want a temperature of around 150°C/300°F.

Using a sharp knife, remove the chicken wing tips, then stretch out the wings and cut the skin in the middle, then crack the joint and open them out flat. Rub the **mix of awesomeness** all over the wings, then place on the barbecue over indirect heat. Cover with the lid and cook for around 50 minutes to 1 hour, or until golden and cooked through. When there's 10 minutes to go, brush over most of the **piri piri sauce**, then continue cooking with the lid on. If the skin needs crisping up a little more, simply remove the lid and move the wings to the direct heat for a few minutes, turning often.

Remove the chicken to a serving platter, brush over more of that awesome piri piri sauce, then serve and enjoy the spicy goodness. Aaaahhhh yeah – these are good!

# BEACH BAR BREAM

TOTAL TIME: 25 MINUTES
PLUS CHILLING

½ a bunch of fresh flat-leaf
parsley, leaves picked

150g unsalted butter, softened

3 cloves of garlic, peeled
and crushed

2 unwaxed lemons

olive oil

2 whole sea bream, gutted, scaled,
fins and gills removed

rock salt

Start by making the flavoured butter. Roughly chop the parsley leaves, then beat in a bowl with the soft butter, garlic and the zest and juice from 1 lemon until well combined (or use a food processor). Spoon the butter on to a large piece of clingfilm, then roll up into an even sausage shape. Twist and fold in the sides, then place in the fridge to chill for at least 30 minutes. Meanwhile, make sure the bars of the grill are really clean and well oiled, then set up your barbecue for the slope technique (see page 10).

Using a small, sharp knife, score the bream four times on each side, then brush with oil and season with plenty of rock salt on both sides. Place directly on the bars near the top of the charcoal slope over a medium-high heat (I like to use a greased fish basket to make them really easy to handle). Grill for around 8 minutes, or until cooked through and the flesh flakes away easily from the bone, turning halfway. Serve the whole bream with a few rounds of flavoured butter, lemon wedges for squeezing over and your favourite greens. The leftover butter is great for any veg, fish or steak – it'll keep for up to 2 weeks in the fridge.

My granddaddy was an avid fisherman and it's from him that my love of fish began. When I was a young tyke, staying with my grandparents down in Virginia Beach, we'd spend the days out fishing in my granddaddy's boat. Then, when I moved to Portugal in the 90s, I watched people grilling fish on the barbecue and it was the best I'd ever tasted. This rad recipe is inspired by one of my all-time favourite joints on the planet, Beach Bar in Burgau, Portugal.

# CHILLI-GLAZED
# LEG OF LAMB

SERVES 8

**TOTAL TIME: 1 HOUR 25 MINUTES**

1 x 2kg leg of lamb,
deboned and butterflied
(get your butcher to do this for you)

4 cloves of garlic, peeled

4 sprigs of fresh rosemary,
leaves picked

olive oil

sea salt and freshly ground
black pepper

**FOR THE GLAZE**

1 fresh red chilli

125ml redcurrant jelly

1 tablespoon dark brown sugar

1½ tablespoons balsamic vinegar

½ teaspoon English
mustard powder

Remove the lamb from the fridge to come up to room temperature. Finely slice the garlic, then with a small, sharp knife, cut a shallow incision into the lamb and carefully push a garlic slice and a couple of rosemary leaves into the opening. Continue making incisions and stuffing with garlic and rosemary all over the surface of the lamb, leaving a 3cm gap between each – you're basically making flavour pockets and, when you're done, it's going to look like a piece of art! Drizzle over a little oil (don't overdo it – the oil can flare up when cooked over direct heat and you don't want to burn your meat) and season with salt and pepper.

Set up your barbecue for the half and half technique (see page 10) – you want a medium-high direct heat. Place a drip tray inside the barbecue on the indirect side. While it's heating up, finely chop the chilli and mix well in a bowl with the rest of the glaze ingredients – how good does that look! Place the leg of lamb over direct heat on the barbecue and cook for around 20 minutes, or until nicely browned and slightly charred, turning every minute or so (if it starts to burn, flip it over). When it's a good colour, move the meat over to the indirect heat, put the lid on like an outdoor oven and cook for around 25 minutes, or until cooked to your liking. When there's about 15 minutes to go, brush over a good coating of that sweet and spicy glaze and continue cooking. Remove to a board to rest for 10 minutes, then slice and serve.

The beauty of a butterflied leg of lamb is you almost halve the cooking time and still get really flavoursome results. This is one of the tastiest dishes I've ever had the pleasure of chompin' on – it's always a crowd-pleaser.

# SLOW & LOW

I cook most of these recipes on my smoker as it's easier to maintain a more consistent heat. I'd really recommend investing in one, but if you don't have one don't let that deter you: these recipes were conceived on my kettle barbecue and it's more than possible to get awesome results using one – it's all about heat maintenance! Good luck and happy eating.

# PULLED BEEF
## WITH GRANDPA'S SAUCE

SERVES
14

**TOTAL TIME: 7 HOURS 30 MINUTES**

1 x 2.5kg piece of beef chuck

1 x **mix of rad** (see page 110)

575ml organic beef stock

**OPTIONAL: GRANDPA'S SAUCE**

2 medium onions, peeled

olive oil

1 clove of garlic, peeled and crushed

½ teaspoon English mustard powder

¼ teaspoon ground cinnamon

1 pinch of ground cloves

500ml passata

1 tablespoon Worcestershire sauce

2 tablespoons cider vinegar

4 tablespoons dark brown sugar

optional: a few drops of
tomato ketchup

**YOU NEED**

1 x disposable foil tray
(roughly 20cm x 30cm)

Remove the beef from the fridge to come up to room temperature. Set up your barbecue for the lonely island technique (see page 11). Place a drip tray inside the barbecue on the indirect side. Cover with the lid, adjust the vents for a nice low heat and allow to heat up like an outdoor oven – you want a temperature of around 110°C/225°F.

Rub the beef all over with the **mix of rad**, pressing it into the flesh with your fingers to ensure it sticks. Place over the indirect heat on the barbecue, cover with the lid and cook for 3 hours, remembering to replenish with hot coals every 45 minutes or so. Transfer the meat to the foil tray, pour in 200ml of stock and cover tightly with extra-strong tin foil. Return to the indirect side of the barbecue for a further 3 hours, or until the meat pulls apart easily. This beef is epic just as it is, so if you want to, go right ahead, pull it apart with two forks now and tuck in. But if you want to do it the way I do it, about 1 hour before the beef's ready, make Grandpa's sauce.

Finely chop the onions and fry in a large pan over a medium heat on the hob with a lug of oil for 5 minutes, or until softened, then add the garlic for a further minute. Reduce the heat to low, stir in the mustard powder, cinnamon and cloves for 30 seconds, then pour in the remaining stock and stir continuously for 1 minute, before adding the rest of the sauce ingredients. Bring to the boil, then reduce to a gentle simmer for about 30 minutes, or until thickened and reduced. Pull the beef apart, then tip into the sauce, along with any juices from the tray, and let the meat and sauce party for a few more minutes. Awesome on a baked potato or used in loads of other dishes, like burritos, tacos and chilli.

My grandpa would stir leftover pulled beef or pork through this sauce, then serve it between two slices of freshly cut bread, with mashed potato spread over one side – the best sandwich ever. Grandpa ruled!

# RADONKULOUS BEEF RIBS

SERVES
6

TOTAL TIME: 4 HOURS

12 short beef ribs, separated,
membrane removed (see tip below)

1 x **Mexican rub**
(see page 106 – leave out the sugar)

200ml American yellow mustard

100ml maple syrup

1 x **BBQ sauce from Planet DAMN**
(see page 120)

Remove the ribs from the fridge to come up to room temperature. Meanwhile, set up your barbecue for the lonely island technique (see page 11). Place a drip tray inside the barbecue on the indirect side. Cover with the lid, adjust the vents for a nice low heat and allow to heat up like an outdoor oven – you want a temperature of around 110°C/225°F.

Rub half the **Mexican rub** all over the ribs. Brush the mustard on top, making sure they're well covered, then sprinkle over the rest of the rub. Place on the barbecue over indirect heat, cover with the lid and cook for around 2 hours, turning halfway and remembering to replenish with hot coals every 45 minutes or so. Divide the ribs between four large pieces of extra-strong tin foil, brush with maple syrup and loosely wrap them up. Return the rib parcels to the barbecue for another 45 minutes to 1 hour with the lid on, or until cooked through and the meat is tender.

Remove the foil parcels to a board, open them up and generously brush over the **BBQ sauce from Planet DAMN**. Add more hot coals to the barbecue and cover to get a medium-low heat rocking – you want a temperature of around 180°C/350°F – then place the ribs directly on the grill, discarding the foil. Cover with the lid and cook for a final 15 to 20 minutes, or until gnarly and caramelized.

★ ☆ ★ ☆ ★ ☆ ★ ☆ ★ ☆ ★ ☆ ★ ☆ ★ ☆ ★ ☆ ★ ☆ ★ ☆ ★ ☆ ★ ☆ ★

Get your butcher to remove the membrane from the ribs – this is a thin, skin-like layer that can prevent all those amazing flavours from soaking in properly.

★ ☆ ★ ☆ ★ ☆ ★ ☆ ★ ☆ ★ ☆ ★ ☆ ★ ☆ ★ ☆ ★ ☆ ★ ☆ ★ ☆ ★ ☆ ★

# PULLED PORK

SERVES
**10**

**TOTAL TIME: 11 TO 17 HOURS**

1 x 3kg piece of higher-welfare
pork shoulder, blade in, skin
and most of the fat removed
(see tip below)

1 x **mix of rad**
(see page 110)

1 x **Hyde County tangy sauce**
(see page 122)

**FOR THE BASTE**

250ml fresh unsweetened
apple juice

75ml fresh unsweetened
pineapple juice

75ml cider vinegar

**YOU NEED**

soaked fruit wood chips
(roughly 300g)

Remove the pork from the fridge to come up to room temperature. Meanwhile, set up your barbecue for the lonely island technique (see page 11). Cover with the lid, adjust the vents for a nice low heat and allow to heat up like an outdoor oven – you want a temperature of around 115°C/240°F.

When the barbecue's ready, mix the baste ingredients and put 125ml into a drip pan, then place inside the barbecue on the indirect side – this will keep the meat really moist (if you're using a smoker, place it in a pot next to the meat). Sprinkle a good handful of wood chips onto the hot coals, then liberally rub the pork all over with the **mix of rad** and place on the barbecue. Cover and cook for 4 to 5 hours, or until a dark mahogany colour (you want it to look black and burnt – this is called the bark). Replenish with hot coals every 45 minutes or so, sprinkling over more wood chips at the same time, for the first 3 hours. Don't be tempted to keep checking it – the less heat you let out, the better!

When the time's up, generously brush the remaining baste all over the pork. Loosely wrap in extra-strong tin foil and cook for at least 5 more hours, or until the meat is soft and easily pulls away from the bone. The longer it cooks the better – a total of 10 hours is good, but 16 hours is what I call butter – it all depends on how much time you have and how hungry you are. Replenish with hot coals every 45 minutes or so. Once ready, rest the meat for 30 minutes, then pull apart with tongs and drizzle over the **Hyde County tangy sauce**. Keep it simple, or serve with my **grilled pineapple salsa** (see page 116), and enjoy the toils of your hard labour.

This is a thick cut of pork that comes from the lower part of the shoulder (known as the pork butt in the US) – always ask for the blade bone in as I think it tastes better cooked that way. If you get it without the blade however, it'll work just as well and you can get away with cooking it for a few hours less, if you like. Save any leftovers for my **pork carnitas** (see page 66).

# PORK CARNITAS

SERVES
6

TOTAL TIME: 1 HOUR 15 MINUTES
PLUS MARINATING

1 x **rainbow slaw** (see page 100)

1 x **grilled pineapple salsa**
(see page 116) or **pico de rado**
(see page 114)

1 x **spicy guacamole** (see page 112)

1 tablespoon **Mexican rub**
(see page 106)

1 teaspoon ground cinnamon

800g leftover **pulled pork**
(see page 64)

24 small soft corn tortillas

vegetable oil

I like to keep this authentic, so set up your barbecue for the slope technique (see page 10), but you can do the whole thing on the hob, if you prefer. While the barbecue's heating up, make the **rainbow slaw** first because it needs to marinate, then get on with the **grilled pineapple salsa** or **pico de rado** and **spicy guacamole**. Mix the **Mexican rub** with the cinnamon, then sprinkle that tasty dust over the pork – you want a nice light coating.

Either divide the tortillas into four stacks of six, wrap each in a double layer of tin foil and warm through on the barbecue for a couple of minutes, or griddle them in a pan on the barbecue with a drizzle of oil for 15 seconds on each side. Meanwhile, preheat a large pan over a direct high heat (or a high heat, if using the hob). Add a drizzle of oil and the pork, then flash fry for around 5 minutes, or until turning crisp around the edges. Remove to a double layer of kitchen paper to drain. Divide the crispy pork, guacamole, salsa and slaw between the tortillas, then tuck in, have fun and get messy.

Using leftover pulled pork in these carnitas (or 'little meats'
in Spanish) is quick, easy and perfect for feeding a crowd.

# CHILLI CON CARNAGE

SERVES
8-10

**TOTAL TIME: 3 HOURS**

olive oil

2 medium onions, peeled

1 bunch of fresh coriander

3 fresh red chillies, deseeded

4 cloves of garlic, peeled

1½ tablespoons ground cumin

2 teaspoons chilli powder

1 teaspoon smoked paprika

1 stick of cinnamon

1kg beef mince

50ml bourbon whisky

1 heaped tablespoon tomato purée

2 x 400g tins of chopped tomatoes

50g dark chocolate (70%) or
1 tablespoon cocoa powder

sea salt and freshly ground
black pepper

2 x 400g tins of kidney beans,
drained and rinsed

**TO SERVE**

basmati rice

soured cream

Set up your barbecue for the slope technique (see page 10). Place a large cast-iron casserole pan on the bars near the top of the charcoal slope, over a medium-high direct heat, and add a good drizzle of oil to the pan. Finely chop the onions and fry for about 5 minutes, or until soft. Meanwhile, finely chop the coriander stalks, keeping the leaves for later, and finely slice 2 chillies and the garlic. Add it all to the pan to fry for a further 2 minutes, then add all the spices, turn up whatever tune you're listening to, and mix everything together.

Move the pan to the top of the slope and the high direct heat. Add the mince, break it up with a wooden spoon and cook for 5 minutes, or until browned all over and any liquid has evaporated. Pour in the bourbon and reduce for a few minutes, then add the tomato purée, chopped tomatoes and two empty tins' worth of water. Break in the chocolate and give it a stir, then season and cover the pan with a lid. Move the pan to the cooler side over a low heat and simmer gently for about 1 hour, stirring occasionally and adding a bit more water if it's drying out too quickly. Stir in the kidney beans and continue simmering for a final 15 to 20 minutes (now's a good time to pop inside and cook your rice), then season the chilli to taste, scatter over the coriander leaves and sliced fresh chilli then serve with steamed rice and a dollop of soured cream. Play Johnny Cash's 'Ring of Fire' and enjoy your fine creation.

> Chilli is good on everything – rice, hot dogs, couscous, corn chips, or try my all-time favourite . . . day-old chilli in an omelette with cheese. It gets better with age.

# SUCKLING PIG

**SERVES 14**

**TOTAL TIME: 7 HOURS**

1 x 5kg higher-welfare suckling pig, internal organs removed

2 small apples

6 unwaxed lemons

6 sprigs of fresh thyme

sea salt and freshly ground black pepper

**YOU NEED**

1 darning needle and butcher's string

soaked fruit wood chips – I like apple (roughly 250g)

Remove the pig from the fridge to come up to room temperature. Meanwhile, set up your barbecue for the lonely island technique (see page 11). Place a drip tray inside the barbecue on the indirect side. Cover with the lid, adjust the vents for a nice low heat and allow to heat up like an outdoor oven – you want a temperature of around 120°C/250°F.

Using a small, sharp knife, score along the length of the pig's skin at 2.5cm intervals. Quarter the apples and halve 3 lemons, then chuck inside the pig with 4 thyme sprigs. Carefully sew the pig up using a darning needle and butcher's string. Squeeze over the juice from the remaining lemons, then rub all over with salt, pepper and the remaining thyme leaves.

Sprinkle a good handful of wood chips over the hot coals. Place the pig over the indirect heat so its back curves around the side of the barbecue. Cover and roast for 5 to 6 hours, or until soft, succulent and the meat falls away from the bone, turning the pig over halfway. To check it's done, stick a thermometer into the thickest part of the leg – once the temperature reaches 85°C/185°F, it's ready. Replenish with hot coals every 45 minutes or so, sprinkling over more wood chips at the same time for the first 3 hours. Once cooked, rest the pig for 30 minutes, loosely covered in tin foil, then carve up and serve – see, it wasn't that difficult!

If you want to get fancy, use an injecting needle to insert a mixture of 250ml of fresh unsweetened apple juice, 75ml of fresh unsweetened pineapple juice, 75ml of cider vinegar and a couple of lugs of Worcestershire sauce into the thickest parts of the pig before cooking. I tend to geek out and do this every time, but it's still awesome without.

# BACON FIREBOMB

SERVES
6-8

TOTAL TIME: 5 HOURS

1kg higher-welfare pork mince

3 tablespoons **mix of rad**
(see page 110)

1 medium red onion, peeled

1 red pepper, deseeded

12 closed cup or
chestnut mushrooms

3 cloves of garlic, peeled

1–2 fresh red or jalapeño chillies

75ml of your favourite BBQ sauce
or my **BBQ sauce from Planet
DAMN** (see page 120)

40 rashers of higher-welfare
smoked streaky bacon

Here's your chance to get
into knitting – only this
time, you'll be weaving
bacon in the construction
of this tasty treat!

Set up your barbecue for the lonely island technique (see page 11). Place a drip tray inside the barbecue on the indirect side. Cover with the lid, adjust the vents for a nice low heat and allow to heat up like an outdoor oven – you want a temperature of around 110°C/225°F. On a piece of greaseproof paper, form the pork mince into a rectangular shape, roughly 2.5cm thick, then sprinkle over the **mix of rad**. Roughly chop the onion, pepper and mushrooms and finely slice the garlic and chillies (keep the seeds in if you like the heat), then spread evenly over the pork rectangle, leaving a 2cm gap around the edge. Drizzle with a few tablespoons of BBQ sauce then, starting with one of the shortest sides, and using the paper to help you, slowly roll it up.

Now for the tricky bit – the bacon weave. Place 8 rashers of bacon side-by-side on a piece of greaseproof paper, then layer over, fold and cross-weave about 12 more rashers to create a lattice, making sure there are no gaps (to see how I do it, check out my Food Tube channel at: youtube.com/djbbq). Repeat with the remaining bacon on a separate piece of greaseproof paper. Pick up one of the greaseproof pieces with the bacon on it, then quickly flip it on to the rolled pork, peel away the paper and gently press down so the bacon is firmly wrapped around one side of the roll. Turn the roll over and do the same again to completely cover the pork in that rad bacon lattice.

Place over indirect heat on the barbecue, cover with the lid and cook for 3 to 4 hours, or until cooked through and gnarly, remembering to replenish with hot coals every 45 minutes or so. When there's about an hour to go, brush over another good drizzle of BBQ sauce. Once done, remove to a board to rest for 10 minutes, then carve into slices (roughly 2.5cm thick) and serve this beautiful house of pork.

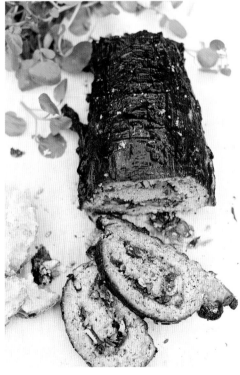

# CHERRY COLA
# SMOKED DUCK

TOTAL TIME: 3 HOURS 40 MINUTES
PLUS MARINATING

1 x 1.3kg whole duck

1 x 330ml can of cherry cola

FOR THE RUB

1 star anise

1 teaspoon coriander seeds

1 teaspoon black peppercorns

½ a cinnamon stick

4 cloves

½ teaspoon chilli powder

1 pinch of sea salt

YOU NEED

soaked wood chips (roughly 300g)

This recipe will impress your friends and their taste buds, and it's pretty damn easy.

Make the rub by toasting all the spices except the chilli powder in a pan over a high heat for 30 seconds, or until smelling incredible. Bash to a fine powder in a pestle and mortar with the chilli powder and salt. Prick the duck skin several times with a fork, then rub the spices really well all over the bird (to really pimp this out, carefully slice and lift the skin off the breast, rub a little more of the mix on to the flesh, then pull the skin back over). Leave to marinate in the fridge for at least 3 hours, or preferably overnight.

Before you start, check if your barbecue lid fits over the duck upright. If not, don't worry, you can lay the bird out flat – you just need to decide which way you're doing it before you prepare the duck, then set the bird aside to come up to room temperature. Meanwhile, set up your barbecue for the lonely island technique (see page 11). Place a drip tray inside the barbecue on the indirect side. Cover with the lid, adjust the vents for a nice low heat and allow to heat up like an outdoor oven – you want a temperature of around 170°C/340°F.

Make sure the cola is at room temperature, then pour out two-thirds of it. Now for the tricky bit – use both hands to pull the duck's rear apart and carefully manoeuvre it on to the can. If you're laying the duck flat, make sure you position the can so the hole is at the top to prevent the cola from spilling out. Sprinkle a good handful of wood chips over the hot coals, then place the bird upright on the middle of the barbecue and cover with the lid. Cook for around 3 hours, or until dark golden and cooked through, rotating halfway. To check if it's ready, pierce a leg with a knife – if the juices run clear, it's done. Replenish with hot coals every 45 minutes or so, sprinkling over some soaked wood chips at the same time. Once cooked, remove the duck to a board to rest for 15 to 20 minutes, then carve up and serve.

# WORLD'S BEST
# MEATLOAF

SERVES
8

TOTAL TIME: 1 HOUR 50 MINUTES

1 large onion, peeled

1 green pepper, deseeded

1 medium carrot, peeled

400g beef mince

400g higher-welfare pork mince

1 clove of garlic, peeled and crushed

1 teaspoon Old Bay Seasoning
or 2 fresh bay leaves, crushed

2 tablespoons Worcestershire sauce

100g stale breadcrumbs

1 teaspoon sea salt

1 teaspoon freshly ground
black pepper

2 large free-range eggs

optional: 150g Cheddar cheese

FOR THE SAUCE

100ml of your favourite BBQ sauce
or my **BBQ sauce from Planet
DAMN** (see page 120)

50ml tomato ketchup

Tabasco sauce

chilli sauce

Set up your barbecue for the heat canyon technique (see page 10). Place a drip tray inside the middle of the barbecue. Cover with the lid and allow to heat up like an outdoor oven – you want a temperature of around 160°C/320°F.

To make your sauce, combine the BBQ sauce and ketchup with a few drops each of Tabasco and chilli sauce, then set aside. Finely dice the onion, pepper and carrot, then put into a large bowl with all the mince, the garlic, bay, Worcestershire sauce, breadcrumbs, salt and pepper. Beat the eggs and add to the mixture, then use your hands to scrunch and mix it all together. Grate in half the cheese (if using), and scrunch to combine.

Remove the mixture to a clean work surface and shape into a rectangular loaf (roughly 25cm in length). Using the handle of a wooden spoon, make four diagonal indents (roughly 1cm deep) into the top of the loaf at 3cm intervals, then pour over half the sauce. Place the meatloaf on a big piece of tin foil or in an old roasting tray, then place on the middle of the barbecue. Cover with the lid and cook for 1 hour to 1 hour 15 minutes, or until cooked through. Grate and sprinkle over the remaining cheese (if using), and continue cooking for a minute or so with the lid on, until melted. Remove to a board to rest for around 10 minutes, then slice it up and serve drizzled with the remaining sauce. Cheers, Grandma!

When my grandma passed away a couple of years ago, my father collected her recipes and made a book for her children, grandchildren and great-grandchildren. This is one of those great family recipes, with some little tweaks by me.

# CLASSIC
# TEXAS BRISKET

**TOTAL TIME: 7 HOURS 45 MINUTES**

2kg beef brisket (see tip below)

1 tablespoon sea salt

1 tablespoon freshly ground
black pepper

optional: 1 teaspoon dried
chilli flakes

**TO SERVE**

fresh white bread

a selection of pickles and
pickled veg

**YOU NEED**

soaked wood chips (roughly 300g)

Set up your barbecue for the heat canyon technique (see page 10). Place a drip tray inside the middle of the barbecue. Cover with the lid, adjust the vents for a nice low heat and allow to heat up like an outdoor oven – you want a temperature of around 110°C/225°F. For this recipe, there's no need to bring the brisket up to room temperature – by cooking it from cold, the meat will absorb more smoke initially and create a nice pink smoke ring just under the surface. You're looking to create a beautiful black crust, called the bark, on the outside. It'll look burnt but don't worry.

Sprinkle a good handful of wood chips over the hot coals. Mix the salt, pepper and chilli flakes (if using), then rub all over the brisket. Place it fat side down on the middle of the barbecue and cook for 4 to 5 hours, or until that gnarly, dark crust forms. Replenish with hot coals every 45 minutes or so, sprinkling over more wood chips at the same time for the first 3 hours.

Wrap the meat in extra-strong tin foil, then cook with the lid on for a further 2 hours, or until tender. Remove to a board to rest in the foil for 30 minutes (or I like to wrap it in a beach towel and place it in a cool box to rest – this will keep the brisket nice and warm). Carve against the grain in thin slices (about 0.5cm thick), then serve with hunks of fresh white bread and all your favourite pickles.

Ask your butcher to leave a thin layer of fat on the brisket, rather than trimming the whole lot off – this will keep the meat from drying out and when caramelized with the spices it just melts in your mouth and turns into what my friend Jason calls Texas foie gras.

# SIDES & SALADS

Man cannot live on meat alone,
though I've tried . . . Lord, I've tried.

# GRILLED PRAWNS WITH MANGO SALAD

SERVES
4

**TOTAL TIME: 30 MINUTES**

1 Romaine lettuce

1 ripe mango

12 large raw king prawns, shells on

rock salt and freshly ground
black pepper

olive oil

100g unsalted butter

juice from 1 lemon

extra virgin olive oil

½ a bunch of fresh flat-leaf parsley,
leaves picked

**YOU NEED**

4 metal or soaked wooden skewers

Set up the barbecue for the half and half technique (see page 10) – you want a medium-high direct heat. Place a drip tray inside the barbecue on the indirect side.

Tear or chop up the lettuce and place in a bowl. Cut the mango halves off the stone, peel the flesh and slice into big, thin slabs, then add to the lettuce and set aside. Remove the prawn shells, leaving the heads and tails intact. Using a small, sharp knife, make a slight incision into the back of the prawns, then open them out slightly and scrape out any black bits (don't butterfly them, but cutting them open slightly will ensure they cook quickly for amazing flavour). Thread 3 prawns on to each skewer, making sure you pierce through each one twice to hold them in place, then season with salt and pepper and drizzle with a little olive oil.

Place the butter and most of the lemon juice in a small cast-iron pan over the indirect heat on the barbecue to melt and have a party. Lay the prawn skewers on the direct heat on the barbecue (I like to use a greased fish basket to make them really easy to handle). Grill for 6 to 10 minutes, or until cooked through and nicely charred, turning halfway. Meanwhile, drizzle a little extra virgin olive oil and a squeeze of lemon juice on to the mango salad, season and toss to coat. Move the prawn skewers to a platter, brush with the lemon butter, then finely chop the parsley and sprinkle over. Tuck in with the mango salad and enjoy the radness!

This is a very new recipe to our household, inspired by a dish we ate last summer at our favourite restaurant on the planet in Portugal. It's the perfect fare on a hot summer's day and an awesome way to start your meal.

# CORN ON THE COB
## WITH MANGO CHILLI BUTTER

**SERVES 6**

TOTAL TIME: 25 MINUTES
PLUS SOAKING

6 corn on the cobs, husks on

1 ripe mango

1 fresh red chilli

1 bunch of fresh coriander,
leaves picked

80g unsalted butter

sea salt and freshly ground
black pepper

1 lime

Set up the barbecue for the half and half technique (see page 10) – you want a medium direct heat.

Keeping the husks intact at the base, carefully pull them back from the cobs, then pull off and discard the stringy silks. Soak in a big bowl of cold water for at least 40 minutes – this will help prevent the husks from burning. Meanwhile, cut the mango halves off the stone, slice each half in a criss-cross shape, then cut off and finely chop the flesh. Finely chop the chilli (keep the seeds in if you like the heat) and the coriander leaves.

Place a small cast-iron pan over the indirect heat on the barbecue and add the butter, mango, chilli and coriander. Stir well until the butter melts, so all those flavours get to know each other. Take the cobs out of the water, pat dry and brush with some mango chilli butter, then pull the husks over to cover (this allows the corn to steam, rather than turning golden straight away). Place on the barbecue over the direct heat, cover with the lid like an outdoor oven and cook for 10 to 12 minutes, turning halfway. Pull back the husks and brush the cobs again with more butter. Keeping the husks pulled back, return the cobs to the direct heat on the barbecue, letting the husks hang over the edge to avoid any big flare-ups. Grill for a further 2 minutes, or until golden and nicely charred, turning frequently, then season to taste with salt, pepper and a good squeeze of lime juice, before biting into your awesome concoction.

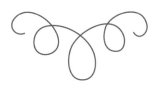

# GRILLED TOMATO SLABS
## FROM PLANET AMAZATRON

**SERVES 6**

**TOTAL TIME: 20 MINUTES**

4 large beef tomatoes

olive oil

1 clove of garlic, peeled and crushed

1 tablespoon extra virgin olive oil

½ a bunch of fresh flat-leaf parsley, leaves picked

½ a bunch of fresh basil, leaves picked

Himalayan pink or sea salt and freshly ground black pepper

Set up your barbecue for the half and half technique (see page 10) – you want a medium-high direct heat.

Slice across the tomatoes so you end up with three equal-sized slabs from each, then arrange cut side up and drizzle with plenty of olive oil. Place cut side down over direct heat on the barbecue for a few minutes, or until bar-marked underneath, then turn over and cook for a further 5 minutes, or until golden (keep checking that they're not burning!). Arrange on a serving platter, then mix the garlic with the extra virgin olive oil and brush over. Finely chop and sprinkle over the herb leaves, then season well with salt and pepper.

I like this with my **Iowa flank skirt steak** (see page 40) being from Planet Amazatron, or my **Grandpa's pulled beef sandwiches** (see tip on page 60), but it goes with just about anything.

# BBQ VEG MEDLEY

SERVES
8

TOTAL TIME: 25 MINUTES

1 head of broccoli

1 cauliflower, outer leaves removed

sea salt and freshly ground
black pepper

3 medium courgettes

250g cherry tomatoes, on the vine

olive oil

1 knob of unsalted butter

6 anchovy fillets

2 cloves of garlic, peeled

1 teaspoon dried chilli flakes

TO SERVE

optional: Parmesan cheese

Set up your barbecue for the half and half technique (see page 10) – you want a medium-high direct heat.

Trim the ends off the broccoli and cauliflower stalks, then slice the heads into 2.5cm thick slabs. Blanch for 1 minute in a pan of boiling salted water over a high heat on the hob, then drain and place in a large bowl. Slice the courgettes lengthways, then add to the bowl with the vine of tomatoes, a drizzle of oil and a pinch of salt and pepper. Toss to coat, then place the veg directly on the barbecue over the direct heat for 10 to 12 minutes, or until soft and nicely charred, turning every few minutes, and removing any veg that are cooked to a big platter as you go.

Meanwhile, place a small cast-iron pan over the indirect heat on the barbecue. Add a lug of oil and the butter, then stir in the anchovies for a couple of minutes until they melt. Finely chop and add the garlic with the chilli flakes and warm gently for a few minutes, stirring occasionally – take care not to burn it!

Remove all the cooked veg to the platter, then pour over the anchovy butter and toss to coat. If you want to take this dish to the next level, finely grate some Parmesan over the top, before serving.

\* \* \* \* \* \* \* \* \* \* \* \* \* \* \* \* \* \* \* \* \* \* \* \* \* \* \* \* \* \*

I've had many people ask if I barbecue anything other than meat, and of course I do. Grilling veg gives them a sweeter taste, and the more I've experimented, the more I've rejoiced in the awesomeness of vegetables.

\* \* \* \* \* \* \* \* \* \* \* \* \* \* \* \* \* \* \* \* \* \* \* \* \* \* \* \* \* \*

# WOODSTOCK DAN'S
# GREEN BEANS

**SERVES 4**

**TOTAL TIME: 15 MINUTES**

1 medium red onion, peeled

1 knob of unsalted butter

olive oil

sea salt and freshly ground
black pepper

300g green beans, trimmed

1 whole nutmeg, for grating

Finely chop the onion. Place the butter and a good drizzle of oil in a large pan over a medium heat (you can do this on the hob or on the barbecue). Once melted, add the onion and a pinch of salt and cook for about 5 minutes, or until soft.

Meanwhile, boil the beans in a pan of boiling salted water for about 4 minutes, or until cooked but with a bit of crunch. Drain and add the beans to the onion pan, followed by a good scraping of nutmeg and a pinch of salt and pepper, then cook for another 6 minutes to really get the party going, stirring occasionally. Have a taste to check you've got the seasoning and the level of radness with the nutmeg right, then serve. Delicious as a side for fish or any meat.

This recipe is inspired by my good friend Woodstock Dan, who used to make big old vats of the stuff at the restaurant where I worked with him back in the late 80s – he let me in on the secret ingredient: nutmeg! It really makes all the difference.

# MEGA STUFFED SWEET POTATOES

SERVES
4

**TOTAL TIME: 1 HOUR 20 MINUTES**

4 large sweet potatoes, scrubbed clean

olive oil

sea salt

optional: 8 rashers of higher-welfare smoked streaky bacon

125g Monterey Jack or Cheddar cheese

4 spring onions, trimmed

1–2 fresh red chillies

**TO SERVE**

soured cream

Set up your barbecue for the heat canyon technique (see page 10). Cover with the lid and allow to heat up like an outdoor oven – you want a temperature of around 175°C/345°F.

Rub the sweet potatoes all over with a drizzle of oil and a good pinch of salt. Place on the middle of the barbecue, cover with the lid and bake for around 1 hour, or until soft in the middle and crisp on the outside. Meanwhile, fry the bacon (if using) in a pan over a high heat (you can do this on the hob) until golden and crisp, then set aside for later.

Split the potatoes open, crumble in the bacon (if using) and grate over the cheese. Return to the indirect heat on the barbecue for a further 5 to 10 minutes with the lid on, or until the cheese has melted. Finely slice the spring onions and chilli then sprinkle them over the potatoes, serve with spoonfuls of soured cream and devour.

# SUPER-DUPER TRIPLY AWESOME
# SMOKED POTATOES

SERVES
8

**TOTAL TIME: 1 HOUR 20 MINUTES**

olive oil

sea salt or rock salt and freshly
ground black pepper

8 medium baking potatoes,
scrubbed clean

**TO SERVE**

soured cream

½ a bunch of fresh chives

**YOU NEED**

soaked wood chips (roughly 150g)

Set up your barbecue for the heat canyon technique (see page 10). Cover with the lid and allow to heat up like an outdoor oven – you want a temperature of around 170°C/325°F.

Sprinkle a good handful of wood chips on to the hot coals. Rub a bit of oil and a pinch of salt and pepper all over each potato, then place on the middle of the barbecue. Cover with the lid and cook for around 1 hour 10 minutes, or until soft in the middle. Turn the potatoes halfway and replenish with hot coals, adding another sprinkling of wood chips at the same time. You can tell if they're done by inserting a sharp knife – if it goes easily through the flesh, you're there. The skin will taste almost sweet with the oil and salt – they're so radelicious.

Split the potatoes open and add a dollop of soured cream to each, then finely chop the chives and scatter over before serving. I also like this with halved cherry tomatoes on top or a simple knob of butter. If you really want to jazz these bad boys up, sprinkle over some **pico de rado** (see page 114) too.

I'd definitely recommend that you make a double batch of these
and use the leftovers to make my **Maryland smoked home fries**
(see page 32) for an awesome breakfast, lunch or dinner.

# MARCO'S STRAWBERRY & SWEETCORN SALAD

SERVES
6

TOTAL TIME: 20 MINUTES

1 corn on the cob

unsalted butter

sea salt and freshly ground
black pepper

3 tablespoons extra virgin olive oil

1½ tablespoons balsamic vinegar

1 Romaine lettuce

1 ripe avocado

juice from ½ a lemon

1 large handful of ripe cherry
tomatoes, on the vine

1 medium cucumber

150g ripe strawberries, trimmed

Set up your barbecue for a medium indirect heat – half and half will work well (see page 10). Place a drip tray inside the barbecue on the indirect side.

Rub the corn cob with a little butter and season with salt, then throw on the barbecue over indirect heat for 12 to 15 minutes, or until nicely charred all over, turning occasionally.

Meanwhile, in a small bowl, whisk together the oil, vinegar and a pinch of salt and pepper. Tear the lettuce into bite-sized pieces or click off the leaves, and arrange on a serving platter. Halve, peel and destone the avocado, slice the flesh, then smother with the lemon juice and scatter over the lettuce. Quarter and add the tomatoes, then halve the cucumber lengthways, scoop out and discard the watery seeds, slice and add to the salad. Halve the strawberries and sprinkle on top. Using a sharp knife, slice the corn kernels off the cob and scatter over the salad, then drizzle the dressing on top, toss gently with your hands and serve.

Here's my version of a recipe inspired by my good friend Marco, from Portugal – he always used to make this for me and it's radeliciously good.

# RAINBOW SLAW

**SERVES 12**

**TOTAL TIME: 20 MINUTES
PLUS MARINATING**

½ a small green or white
cabbage (400g)

½ a small red cabbage (400g)

1 medium red onion, peeled

3 large carrots, peeled

2 raw beetroots, peeled

2 crisp green apples, cored

½ a bunch of fresh coriander,
leaves picked

125ml fresh unsweetened
apple juice

125ml cider vinegar

125ml extra virgin olive oil

1 teaspoon sea salt

Finely shred all the veg and cut the apples into matchsticks, or coarsely grate it all, then roughly chop the coriander leaves and put it all into a bowl. Add the apple juice, vinegar, oil and salt and mix well to combine. Cover with clingfilm and leave to marinate in the fridge for about 1 hour so the veg can soak up all that rad flavour. Take it out, give it all another mix up, then serve.

This is clean, refreshing and totally awesome.

This makes a great side to just about anything, is rad chucked in a wrap, and awesome with my **pork carnitas** (see page 66).

# GRILLED LETTUCE
## WITH BLUE CHEESE DRESSING

SERVES
6

TOTAL TIME: 15 MINUTES

sea salt and freshly ground
black pepper

8 rashers of higher-welfare
pancetta or smoked streaky bacon

6 baby gem lettuces

olive oil

FOR THE DRESSING

100g blue cheese

1 lemon

1 small clove of garlic, peeled
and crushed

2 tablespoons soured cream

6 tablespoons extra virgin olive oil

2 tablespoons cider vinegar

Set up your barbecue for the slope technique (see page 10). Meanwhile, crumble the blue cheese into a clean jar, then add a squeeze of lemon juice and the rest of the dressing ingredients. Put the lid on, shake vigorously to mix, then season to taste.

Place the pancetta or bacon directly on the barbecue over a medium-high heat. Grill for 4 to 5 minutes, or until crispy, then set aside to cool. Halve each lettuce lengthways, keeping the root intact, then brush with a little olive oil, season with salt and pepper and place cut side down over a high heat. Cook for a couple of minutes, or until bar-marked underneath, then turn and cook for another minute, or until charred but with a nice crunch.

Transfer the grilled lettuces to a platter, drizzle with the blue cheese dressing, crumble over the crispy pancetta or bacon, then serve.

My wife kept asking me when I was going to cook something other than meat for once, so I tweaked this recipe for her to make it veggie – simply replace the bacon with 50g of roughly chopped, toasted pecans or walnuts, tossed in maple syrup.

# Rubs,

# DIPS, SALSAS

# & SAUCES

Every rockstar needs a roadie and
every main dish deserves the same.

# MEXICAN RUB

**5 TABLESPOONS**

TOTAL TIME: 5 MINUTES

1 tablespoon soft dark brown sugar

1 tablespoon sea salt

1 tablespoon ground cumin

1 tablespoon chilli powder

1 teaspoon onion granules

1 teaspoon garlic granules

1 teaspoon cayenne pepper

1 teaspoon hot smoked paprika

Heat, tang and earthiness put the roots of this rub firmly in Mexico. Throw all the ingredients into a bowl and mix well, breaking up any lumps of sugar with the back of a spoon. Use straight away on my **pork carnitas** (see page 66) or **party-time chicken fajitas** (see page 34), or store in an airtight container for a few months, ready to use when you like. It works great on chicken, fish or beef.

This awesome rub is also what you need for my **radonkulous beef ribs** (see page 62), but for that you don't need as much sweetness so just leave the sugar out, and add 1 tablespoon of freshly ground black pepper into the mix instead.

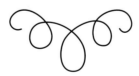

This rub is super-hot or, as my mom would say, hotter than a goat's butt in a chilli pepper patch! But if you want to mellow out the heat, just use 1 teaspoon of chilli powder.

# MIX OF AWESOMENESS

**TOTAL TIME: 15 MINUTES**

zest from ½ an unwaxed lemon

zest from ¼ of an unwaxed orange

3 tablespoons soft dark
brown sugar

1 tablespoon sea salt

1 tablespoon freshly ground
black pepper

1 tablespoon onion granules

1 tablespoon garlic granules

1 teaspoon smoked paprika

optional: 1 teaspoon chilli powder

Sweet, smoky, zesty and just the right side of tang, this is pure awesomeness. Preheat the oven to 110°C/225°F/gas ¼. Scatter the lemon and orange zest onto a sheet of greaseproof paper on a baking tray and bake for 10 minutes, or until lightly golden and any moisture has evaporated. Put 2 teaspoons of the dried zest into a bowl, then throw in the rest of the ingredients. If you're feeling daring, add the chilli powder too, then mix well and it's ready to use on my **cherry wood smoked chicken** (see page 18), **ballistic BBQ chicken** (see page 38) or **piri piri chicken wings** (see page 52).

This also tastes awesome on fish and vegetables. It goes with anything really – my friend Ed Macfarlane (the lead singer of Friendly Fires) keeps a tub by his bedside table and dips raw carrots into it as a snack. It's good!!

I like to make a double or triple batch of this – it'll last for a good few months, stored at room temperature in an airtight container, ready to use whenever you like.

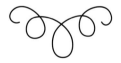

# MIX OF RAD

**8 TABLESPOONS**

TOTAL TIME: 5 MINUTES

2 tablespoons soft dark
brown sugar

1 heaped tablespoon sea salt

1 tablespoon freshly ground
black pepper

1 tablespoon ground cumin

1 tablespoon ground coriander

1 tablespoon onion granules

1 tablespoon garlic granules

½ teaspoon mustard powder

optional: ½ teaspoon chilli powder

optional: ½ teaspoon dried
chilli flakes

The mix of rad is a deep, sweet, earthy rub with a bit of a kick. You can maintain that level of heat by playing with the chilli powder and chilli flakes – if you don't like hot food, then don't use them. If you think you can handle it, I sometimes throw in 1 teaspoon of each! Sometimes I like to add ½ a teaspoon of ground cloves too, so if you've got them, throw them in as well.

To make this mix, simply place all the ingredients in a bowl, give it a good mix up and it's ready to go. This is killer on my **pulled pork** (see page 64), **pulled beef** (see page 60), **bacon firebomb** (see page 72) and **awesomeatron lamb loin chops** (see page 46), as well as on burgers, bacon, chicken, lamb and, according to a friend of mine, in cheese toasties!

Just like my **mix of awesomeness** (see page 108), I like to make an extra big batch of this stuff. I do it with my **Mexican rub** (see page 106) too, so I've always got all my rubs and mixes jarred up and ready to use, whenever I need them.

# SPICY GUACAMOLE

SERVES 4–6

TOTAL TIME: 15 MINUTES

4 ripe avocados

2 ripe plum tomatoes

1 bunch of fresh coriander, leaves picked

1 fresh red chilli

juice from 1 lime

juice from ½ a lemon

sea salt and freshly ground black pepper

You'll need a large bowl, as this can be quite messy (I destroy the kitchen every time I cook, so it is for me!). Halve and destone the avocados, then scoop the flesh into the bowl. Chop the tomatoes, finely chop the coriander leaves and finely slice the chilli (keep the seeds in if you like the heat), then add it all to the bowl. Squeeze in the lime and lemon juice, then mix and mash with a fork – you want a thick, chunky consistency that'll hold on well to a corn chip (see how to make them in my **pico de rado** recipe on page 114). Season to taste with salt and pepper and voilà! This goes brilliantly with my **party-time chicken fajitas** (see page 34) and **kick-ass fish tacos** (see page 20), or is great simply as a rad snack.

Having a good guacamole recipe is a must in anyone's cooking repertoire. I still clearly remember the first time I dipped a corn tortilla chip into a bowl of guac: my life changed. It's too long a story to go into here, but basically it involves an ex-girlfriend gone bad. The moral of that story would be – when the girl freaks on you, make guacamole and learn to fly . . .

# PICO DE RADO

SERVES
6

TOTAL TIME: 15 MINUTES

5 ripe plum tomatoes

1 medium red onion, peeled

½ a bunch of fresh coriander

1 fresh red chilli, deseeded

juice from 1–2 limes

sea salt and freshly ground
black pepper

Chop the tomatoes into small chunks (some people like to scoop out the seeds, but I use everything) and finely chop the onion. Finely chop the coriander leaves (you can use a few stalks too, if you like), and finely slice the chilli (keep the seeds in if you like the heat), then throw all that raw radness into a bowl. Add the lime juice – it's up to you if you use one or two, but in my opinion, the more lime the better to make this super-addictive. Season to taste with salt and pepper, then mix well.

Serve with tacos or burritos, or as a snack with tortilla chips. I like to make my own by cutting corn tortillas into triangles, then frying them in vegetable oil for a minute or two, until golden, turning halfway – you can't beat that awesome crunch.

I've taken the fresh Mexican salsa, pico de gallo, and upped the rad factor with some heat, but you can easily leave the chilli out and keep it classy if you prefer.

# GRILLED PINEAPPLE SALSA

SERVES
6

1 medium pineapple

250g ripe cherry tomatoes, on the vine

1 fresh red chilli

1 bunch of fresh coriander, leaves picked

juice from 1 lime

sea salt

Set up your barbecue for the half and half technique (see page 10) – you want a high direct heat.

Top and tail the pineapple, then slice off the skin. You now need to create nice slabs of fleshy fruit, so chop it off in big rectangles, roughly 2cm thick, then throw away the core. Grill the pineapple slabs on both sides, until turning golden, then remove to a plate and let those slabs of rad cool right down.

Meanwhile, quarter the tomatoes, finely chop the chilli (keep the seeds in if you like the heat) and roughly chop the coriander leaves. Once cool, finely chop the grilled pineapple then mix it with the other chopped ingredients and add it to a bowl. Squeeze over the lime juice, give it all a mix and season to taste with salt. Now, bask in your awesomeness and enjoy this amazing salsa. I like to make big bowls of it to go with chilli, corn tortillas, tacos or my **pulled pork** (see page 64).

When you nail this recipe, you can dub yourself a 'condimelier' – someone who is an expert in the art of creating awesome condiments.

# MAD MANGO SALSA

**SERVES 4-6**

TOTAL TIME: 15 MINUTES

1 ripe mango

½ a medium red onion, peeled

½ a cucumber

1 bunch of fresh coriander,
leaves picked

juice from 1 lime

sea salt

Cut the mango halves off the stone and slice each half in a criss-cross shape. Cut off and finely chop the flesh with the onion, cucumber and coriander leaves, then scrape into a bowl. Squeeze in the lime juice and mix well. Season to taste with salt, before serving.

I've always been a huge **fish taco** fan and they go rad with this recipe. Check 'em out on page 20. I used to interview a lot of big metal and rock bands from the States and I always asked what they missed about America. The answer would always end up at fish tacos, and that's the inspiration behind this salsa – it's easy, refreshing and perfect with a taco. The fruit and fish are like brothers. If a fish taco was a pro-snowboarder, this mango salsa would be his best shred buddy.

# BBQ SAUCE FROM PLANET DAMN

MAKES 600ML

**TOTAL TIME: 1 HOUR 20 MINUTES**

1 medium onion, peeled

3 garlic cloves, peeled

1 Scotch bonnet chilli, deseeded

1 fresh red chilli, deseeded

50g unsalted butter

olive oil

1 tablespoon runny honey

2 tablespoons soft dark brown sugar

1 teaspoon English mustard powder

2 tablespoons Worcestershire sauce

3 tablespoons tomato purée

1 swig of bourbon whisky

2 tablespoons dark soy sauce

3 tablespoons white wine vinegar

125ml tomato ketchup

a few drops of Tabasco sauce

3 fresh bay leaves

sea salt and freshly ground black pepper

Finely chop the onion, garlic and chillies. Melt the butter with a good drizzle of oil in a medium pan over a medium heat (you can do this on the hob or on the barbecue), then add the onion, garlic and chilli, and cook for 7 to 10 minutes, or until soft but not coloured, stirring occasionally.

Now you can start adding in more radness. Stir in the honey, sugar and mustard powder until smooth and well combined – you want to make sure these dudes get to know one another real good. Stir in the remaining ingredients (except the salt and pepper), followed by 200ml of water to loosen it up. Bring everything to the boil, then reduce the heat and simmer for 45 minutes to 1 hour, or until thickened and reduced – if it gets too thick, add a little more water to loosen, then season to taste. Strain into a bowl and use straight away, or store in sterilized jars in the fridge for up to 2 weeks.

Congrats! You've just made your own BBQ sauce from scratch and this one's from Planet DAMN. Time to wake the neighbours, walk the dog and have a big old party.

I made this sauce to go with my **radonkulous beef ribs** (see page 62), but it works really well on all types of meat and is awesome on burgers.

# HYDE COUNTY TANGY SAUCE

MAKES 750ML

**TOTAL TIME: 50 MINUTES**

1 medium onion, peeled

1 tablespoon vegetable oil

1 knob of unsalted butter

100ml cider vinegar

65ml fresh unsweetened apple juice

1 heaped teaspoon light brown sugar

½ teaspoon dried chilli flakes

1 teaspoon sea salt

1 teaspoon freshly ground black pepper

½ an unwaxed lemon

½ a bunch of fresh coriander

Finely chop the onion. Place a large pan over a medium heat (you can do this on the hob or on the barbecue), then add the oil and butter. Once melted, add the onion and cook for 5 minutes, or until softened. Pour in the vinegar, apple juice and 350ml of water and bring to the boil. Reduce to a simmer, then chuck in the sugar, chilli flakes, salt and pepper. Stir well until the sugar dissolves into the abyss of awesomeness.

Slice the lemon into rounds, then stir into the sauce. Finely slice and add the coriander stalks (keep the leaves to use in another dish). Cook for 30 to 35 minutes so all those flavours can enjoy the party, mixing occasionally to keep them stoked. Remove from the heat and pour through a sieve into a bowl to use straight away, or store in an airtight container in the fridge for up to 2 weeks. Delicious with my **pulled pork** (see page 64), or shredded chicken or lamb.

This recipe is inspired by my good friend and intelligent dude Rodney Bryant, from Hyde County, North Carolina. The style of barbecuing in Carolina is very different from Texas and the Midwest – it's all about the tang! I've taken on what Rod taught me and thrown in some rad new flavours.

# PIRI PIRI SAUCE

**TOTAL TIME: 15 MINUTES**

8 fresh red malagueta or piri piri chillies (use regular red chillies if you need to)

3 cloves of garlic, peeled

180ml olive oil

50ml cider vinegar

2 tablespoons bourbon whisky

juice from ½ a lemon

1 teaspoon sea salt

If you have a blender you can use that to mix up this rad concoction, otherwise get all feral and just chop and mix. Wearing gloves, halve the chillies lengthways and scrape out the seeds (or keep them in for über heat), then finely slice and put into a bowl. Finely slice the garlic and add to the bowl with the remaining ingredients. Mix well, then use straight away to make my **piri piri chicken wings** (see page 52), or store in sterilized bottles or jars in the fridge for up to 6 months. My good friend Adriano Shepherd says, 'You need to let this brew and do its thing for at least 2 weeks before using.' Adriano owns one of my top-five restaurants on this planet, Beach Bar, so I'd heed his advice. Now go find the closest mirror and tell yourself: 'You are an awesome person.'

This recipe is inspired by the Lagos region of Portugal, where I spent three summers working and which I still visit every year. There are loads of local versions of the sauce, but I've adapted the recipe by adding bourbon whisky to give it a bit of Southern US flair.

# ★ THANKS

First off, I want to thank my family for putting up with my shenanigans – Naya, Blue, Noah, Frasier and Crosby (the dog). I love y'all so much. The pizza dough recipe is Naya's, who helped a lot with this book – so thanks, honeypot pie. A major thanks goes out to my dad, Ron Stevenson, for trusting me to barbecue dinner when I was a little whippersnapper, and thanks to both sets of grandparents, who taught me so much about food – not only cooking it but enjoying it. My mom, Ruby – thanks for letting me get stuck in when you cooked your southern-style food, and my step-mom, Pam – you've been the raddest person on the planet, thanks for buying me my first snowboard back in '85!

Huge props go out to Jamie Oliver for believing in me – thank you so much for all the opportunities you've thrown my way. Charlie Clapp, the food stylist for this book, worked her little belly off – you rule beyond ruling! David Loftus, you're the superhero of photographers – I'm off to buy you a cape for your next journey. Thanks big time, bro-dawg! Mark Parr, aka Lord Logs, thanks for teaching me so much about wood. Ha, I said 'wood'. Helen Raison and everyone at Weber UK, thanks for supplying me with my favourite barbecues ever – you catz are amazing! A very special thanks goes out to my designer, Alice Vandy – thanks for custom-building my spandex catsuits; I know my torso isn't the easiest to work with. Dan Sacharoff, aka Woodstock Dan, for teaching me so many rad recipes and for letting me crash on your hammock back in Ocean City, Maryland – you are missed, my old friend. Rebecca Rubs Walker and Malou Herkes, my editors on this book, who had to put up with a lot of radiculous made-up words – thank you so much for being patient with my severe lack of focus.

Damn, I need to watch my word count here. In no particular order, here we go. Thank you . . .

Kings of Leon, Toby Millage, Elliott Chaffer and family, Tim Warwood, Adam Kaleta, Hank Sender, Nicole Campbell, Wayne Yates, Marc Churchill, Graeme and Nina Hawkins, Built to Spill, Zoe Collins, Brian Newton, Rodney Bryant, Edd and Imogen Martin, Jack Bibbo, Will Hughes, DC Shoes, Jim Wedlake, Ed Leigh (Satanwhoppercock), Geoff Glendenning, Adriano Shepherd, Marco Shepherd, Catarina Shepherd, the Beach Bar in Burgau, Jo Ralling, Ken Block, The Cure, Matt Shaw, Beth Stevenson Lee, Chris Lee, Avery and Noelle, Ralph Nordile (best step-dad ever), Rich Herd, Paul Casey, Emily Taylor, Paul Bussey, Tamsin McGee (thanks for the rad logo and the rest), Tim Woolcott, Dinosaur Jr., Annie Lee and Caroline Pretty